I0840999

# THE RELATIONS OF WOMEN TO CRIME

BY

ELY VAN DE WARKER, M. D.

ISBN-13:
978-1727163339

ISBN-10:
1727163338

## I.

THE first traditional crime, the fratricide of Abel, was a natural outgrowth from the conditions of society, which, compared to the present relations of civilized men, existed germ-like around him. These conditions alone gave motive and direction to the deed. To all the after-centuries of human crime this primal offense has existed as a type. Both in cause and effect it is reduced to its simplest proportions. The criminal represents the retrograde tendency of society; the savagism which exists in every community. Order and progress are preserved by an irrepressible conflict waged on the border-land, as it were, of civilization. Many of these crimes grow out of the artificial wants of society. Others are but relative and belong to particular conditions, or orders of men, and at other times and places are without meaning and void of offense. Thus society is ever eager for the warfare, and, at the time it creates the crime, prepares the weapons for its punishment.

The propensity to crime is a fixed element in human nature. Quetelet, whom I have frequently referred to in the course of these papers, has with singular sagacity and perseverance reduced the social relations of man nearly to an exact science. The dark and tortuous by-ways in life, which so many seem perforce to follow, arrange themselves with the regularity of geometrical lines under the clear illumination of his analysis. Yet these are surface-lines only. There are profound depths of human misery and crime, over which a veil seems drawn by a merciful hand, and in which we have but a suspicion of the force of law. But, in these depths, in which the terminal fibres of human relations find soil and sustenance, can be found the origin of the ordinances under which these surface-lines are grouped. If this he so, it follows that crime must be studied as a natural phenomenon rather than as an accident. Those efforts which society has made to stamp out and confine this tendency to evil must, to an equal extent, spring from higher law; just as a breakwater is reared to protect an exposed harbor from the encroachments of storm and wave.

We have of late years come to look upon criminals as a special class of the community. We have come to complacently call them the "criminal class," just as we do the mercantile class or any other reputable order of men. This is so far true as to be capable of proof more by the exceptions than the rule. We have come to look upon crime as we do the typhus fever or the cholera, as prevailing mainly amid dirt and ignorance. I believe this to be true only so far as ignorance permits those good qualities in men to be undeveloped which require culture for their development; and the existence of such qualities has not as yet been demonstrated. It must be understood that while the word "ignorance" does not express a positive quantity, it yet expresses a positive quality which is true of the mass of people. This word with perfect fairness may be applied to the vast numbers which swell the aggregate of a census-table, without any qualification. I believe it can be shown that it is simply from excess in numbers that the ignorant classes furnish the recruits to the ranks of crime, and not from any tendency to crime dependent upon the negative quality of ignorance. A careful analysis of facts in this field induces Mr. Buckle to say that "the existence of crime, according to a fixed and uniform scheme, is a fact more clearly attested than any other in the moral history of man."[1] Another high authority may be quoted in evidence to prove that this scheme is exempt from those laws which govern intellectual development: "It is one of the plainest facts that neither the individuals nor the ages that have been most distinguished for intellectual achievements have been most distinguished for moral excellence, and that a high intellectual and material civilization has often coexisted with much depravity."[2]

All this seems to show us that there is a rhythm in human actions that forms a minor chord in the forever unwritten music which those who love Nature know as existing profoundly in all her works.

Since we are dealing with an element in human character which preserves a fixed value, it is evident that we may study the relation of any class in any community to these constantly-recurring phenomena, provided we can isolate this class from all others. In the study before us, this has already been done by the division of mankind into the sexes. I need draw no other line. Women stand out so clearly as a class, and, in relation to any series of acts which preserve a more or less constant periodicity, are so sharply defined from man, that they are easily contrasted with him in relation to any condition common to both.

I have already called attention to the fact that intellectual development obeys other laws than those which relate to crime. This requires to be brought out more clearly in relation to women. In this age women are receiving more chivalric attention, more material respect, than in any other known to history. In this century they are accorded the full right, and are given the aid of some of the best intellects among the other sex, to adjust those wrongs under which they have labored for ages. They are identified with every scheme of love and purity which demands good motives and a sympathy that never slumbers. It is for this reason, then, that, when we associate women with the idea of crime, it is difficult to believe that they are not influenced by other laws than those which affect men. There is nothing in a brawny hand and coarse muscle which tends to evil. The hand which executes may be white and begemmed. The mind which plans may be cultivated and refined.

In the study before us, we shall be obliged to resort to other facts than those simply contained in tabulated statements of crime. Statistics has done much in social study, and in this instance it has pointed out the existence of law in human action in the aggregate; but it has gone no deeper. We can

establish by its means a probable difference
in the degree to which the sexes are affected
by crime; we can so group these numerical
statements that they will be a mutual check
upon each other, but if we are to learn any
thing of the under stratum of human life, of
its curves and faults, of which we see only
here and there an upheaval upon the surface
of society, we must study sexual and general
character, we must observe the mutual
relation and dependence of the sexes and
classes upon each other, and give due credit
to the cerebral and physical differences
which go to make up the sum of sex all of
which are beyond the province of figures to
express. In the course of these papers,
therefore, I shall resort to statistics only to
the extent I have mentioned. The popular
character which I have endeavored to give
them also forbids the resort to statistical
detail, except to the extent which is
inseparable from the nature of the study.

As in hygiene so in crime, there is not one
law for woman and another for man. The
emotions which impel to crime are few, and
to the operation of which the sexes are both
exposed. But, it does not follow that these
causes react in the production of crime to an
equal degree. The propensity to crime, as
defined by its actual commission, is four

times as great in men as in women.[3] Here at the outset we are confronted by a remarkable contrast. But, allowed to stand as here stated, it involves a vital error. A propensity to crime is its existence latent in the possibilities of the individual. Justin McCarthy, in one of his novels, in describing a character defines her virtue as purely anatomical while mentally most unchaste. Here the propensity was one thing and its physical expression another. It therefore follows that if we are to reach the degree of woman's propensity to crime it must be by other means than a simple expression of the difference in the actual perpetration of total crime. The propensity can be approximately measured by the degree of the offense. Quality and degree are in law the measures of the punishment inflicted on the offender. This is called justice, and it is indeed tempered with mercy when we compare it with the operations of law less than a century ago, when it dealt with crime simply as a quality without reference to degree. In its treatment of criminals, society took its first scientific stand-point when it measured the propensity to evil by the degree of evil actually committed. It seems safe to assume that in a certain limited range, as the degree of crime defines its penalty, so also it expresses the

extent of the propensity. Another fact may
be approximately established from the same
data. The causes of crime, those deeply-
hidden undercurrents existing in society, the
ebb and flow of which seem to register
themselves in undeviating curves of human
conduct, must vary in intensity to the degree
of crime which is their natural outgrowth.
Thus, a man who commits a criminal act
with the full knowledge that his life is
jeopardized thereby must surely be exposed
to an influence far greater than one who,
under all circumstances, would shrink from
the greater crime through a sense of
punishment, but would not hesitate to
commit a lesser offense. If this is not so,
then society has been acting upon a false
theory in its repression of crime by the fear
of punishment. But I believe legislation for
this purpose has been based upon a correct
knowledge of human nature, and that the
average man with criminal tendencies is, to
a certain degree, deterred from criminal
conduct by a fear of punishment. There is
strong confirmation of this in the condition
of society existing in the border States and
raining regions, in which there is a low
estimate of the value of human life, not from
the fact that life is individually less precious
there than elsewhere, but that the tendency
to this form of crime exists in greater force

11

as a natural outcome of the conditions under which human life is there grouped. I believe it is just, therefore, to partly form an estimate of the tendency to crime by the method I have adopted, aided by a simple comparison of the prevalence of crime in general in the sexes.

The apparent great excess in the prevalence of crime among men forms one of the most interesting facts of sex in crime. At the outset we ought to reach, if possible, the cause. In this connection all ideas of the innate morality of women over men must be abandoned. Modern literature is full of a false and even morbid idea upon this subject. M. Michelet has written a romance called "Woman,"[4] and it is a fair sample of what may be termed the sentimental estimate of the. sex. But the frail creature portrayed in the florid sentences of Michelet is not the woman of France. One glance at the tables of Quetelet proves this.

We must take a practical view of woman's character. She must be regarded as one in whom the passions burn with as intense heat as in the other sex. The limits of her morality are the same as man's. She attains purity in the same manner; and she meets sexual disaster through the same means. Her

12

worldly view is bounded by the same horizon. She upholds for herself the same standard of success or failure. Temptations run in the same channel and are resisted by the same psychical traits. The forces of heredity play the some role in her mental and bodily life. Beyond these, she belongs to a different mental type from man, the effects of which in our present knowledge, and in the relations we are now studying the sex, reach limits impossible to fix. I can see no other way of viewing the sex, and reaching any thing like approximate truth in her relations to crime.

In crimes against persons in which personal strength forms an element, there is a physical factor for the difference. The ratio of strength between the sexes is as sixteen to twenty-six, and this is found to correspond to the difference in which women and men participate in crimes against persons and property.[5] Such a coincidence as this, constantly recurring, renders, in this broad classification of crimes in general, such an explanation probable. But, in a closer analysis of crime in particular, this physical basis loses its value as a probable cause. While we must allow that sexual difference in strength finds a reflex result in consciousness, and thus places a limit to the

13

acts of either sex, yet in crimes against persons we find the sexes approaching to and receding from a common ratio. It is this fact which leads me to the conclusion that all argument regarding the innate excess of moral qualities in the female sex over the male, is based upon a fallacy. It is strongly confirmatory of this, that a simple numerical comparison of the prevalence of crime in the sexes leads to error, unless we credit women with the fewer temptations, the less opportunity, and those forms of sexual cerebration which find their expression in a want of belligerence which characterize women. Thus it would be obviously wrong to assert that, because twelve women to one hundred men are convicted of assassination, women represent more than eight times the morality of men in relation to this one offense. This crime is just the one to call into play all those conditions which constitute the moral atmosphere and conditions of sex. Woman's want of opportunity, the nature of her occupations, and the absence of the same degree of temptation, must all be taken into consideration in forming an opinion of the moral equivalent of women in connection with the crime. If it were possible to give to each one of these modifying conditions a numerical expression, this moral equivalent

could be given a mathematical value. But
this is impossible, and each possesses in
itself an imaginary yet appreciable value.
Again, let us group all those crimes against
persons which involve the taking of human
life, and observe the extent to which the
sexes are engaged. For all crimes against
persons, Quetelet places the ratio at sixteen
to one hundred; but in the class of crimes I
have selected, involving infanticide,
poisoning, parricide, assassination, and
murder, we find this ratio nearly doubled,
being thirty to one hundred. It is evident that
woman's tendency to crime must be
measured by some other standard than
innate morality. If we apply to these figures
the theory that the degree of crime is in a
measure the test of propensity, we obtain
some startling results. Take the felonies
named above in the aggregate, and while the
marked difference of sex in the commission
of total crime is evident, we see that in the
perpetration of these grave offenses she
exceeds her ratio of crimes against property.
I think this shows the probability that those
emotions or passions which serve as the
incentives to crime, approach in intensity the
same mental conditions in the other sex.
When we consider the strong emotional
nature of women, and that many of these
emotions are of an organic or sexual origin,

and their social relations, and the habit of dependence, which they have inherited, upon these relations, we must admit that the moral elements of crime are so strengthened as to modify materially their deficiencies of strength and want of opportunity.

Many of woman's social relations are well calculated to clear and make easy the way to crime. It is another confirmation of the fact that society prepares the crime, and the criminal executes it. Compensation is found for her in the fact that society also places obstacles in her way by removing many temptations and opportunities for offense. But, in those crimes which are the natural outgrowth of her sexual and social relations, we find woman standing upon man's own level as a criminal. Thus, in infanticide and in poisoning, both of which, from the degree of offense involved, show a strong action of the exciting cause, all sexual difference in numbers disappears, and it is evident that the tendencies to those two crimes are equivalent in the sexes.

As the preceding shadows forth the interesting fact that woman, as a criminal, is under forces of both restraint and non-restraint other than sexual differences of mind or body, compared to man, it will be necessary to refer briefly to the nature and extent of these modifying circumstances, in order to appreciate the true bearings of the question. These conditions spring mainly from her social relations. This leaves us another important class of modifying conditions which may be traced to sexual relations. Two classes can therefore be made: (*A*) social conditions, and (*B*) sexual conditions, modifying woman's relation to crime.

The first (*A*) which exist sufficiently near to the subject to call for analysis are: (1) occupation, (2) opportunity, and (3) marriage; and each of which must have a marked influence on sporadic cases of crime, and especially upon the creation of the criminal habit. But, much as these modifying circumstances have to do with the question before us, yet returns involving these particulars are so imperfect that we are able to get but a hint of the extent to which each acts.

(1.) Occupation, as it places woman above temptation to the minor degrees of crime, or as it brings her more closely in contact with constantly-recurring temptations, becomes an important factor. It is evident that these conditions must exist in the lives of both

17

sexes, and have their influence on the frequency of crime and the nature of the offense. Thus in an official return[6] quoted by Quetelet, in which the offenders are classified by occupation, the accused of the eighth class who all exercised liberal professions, or enjoyed a fortune, are those who have committed the greatest number of crimes against persons; while eighty-seven hundredths of the accused of the ninth class, composed of people without character, as beggars and prostitutes, have attacked scarcely any thing but property. When the accused are divided into two classes, one of the liberal professions, and the other composed of journeymen, laborers, and servants, this difference is rendered still more conspicuous.[7] This is sufficient to render the broad inference probable that want or necessity induces but the minor degrees of crime against property, while the more serious phases of crime belong to the opposite conditions of society, or have their mainspring in other motives. In the *Compte Général de l'Administration de la Justice,* the occupation of the accused is given by sex, and under the article *Domestiques* we find one hundred and forty-nine men and one hundred and seventy-five women employed as personal servants, nearly all of whom were accused of the minor degrees of

crimes against property. These proportions
for this occupation hold about the same
relations from year to year. As persons so
engaged are maintained generally by their
employers, want could not have existed as a
motive for these offenses. Cupidity, or the
desire to appear well, with the facility of its
gratification, afforded by occupation, is the
probable motive, and, making allowance for
the slight excess of women so employed,
exists in almost equal intensity in both
sexes.

From what we know of the inadequate pay
attending many of the employments in
which women are engaged, it is safe to say
that irresistible temptation is often the result.
In the larger cities there are thousands of
women, reaching from youth to advanced
life, who are but just able to provide
themselves with the necessities of life by
labor extending over more than half of the
hours in the day. Many of these have others
dependent upon them, which must add very
much to the tendency to the minor forms of
crime. But the tendency to crime arising
from inadequate pay is twofold. It may not
be sufficient to meet necessary bodily wants,
or barely sufficient, or, as is too generally
the case, it is insufficient to supply those
matters of personal adornment and comforts

of surrounding, small as many of them are,
which are so necessary to contentment. This
tendency to adornment either in person or
surroundings must be looked at seriously as
a sexual mental trait in women. They need
but to reach the rudimentary stage of
education to have developed in them
æsthetic tendencies, and which in many
seem to exist innately. This feeling is also
closely allied to that personal pride which is
such a safeguard against the encroachments
of vice. This pride of person is to many a
struggling woman what a moral atmosphere
is to others. To the one it is an instinct which
keeps her from the degradation, and that
conduct which leads to it; to the other it is
the moral force which surrounds her and
lifts her above the opportunities for evil.
Viewed in this light, personal pride, as
expressed in the adornment of person and
home, may replace the purely moral sense to
a certain extent. But pushed beyond the
point at which it contributes to correct
conduct, and allowed to exist solely as a
sexual trait, it may become a strong
incentive to crime. There is no reason to
doubt but it is mainly the cause which makes
crimes against property so nearly equal in
the sexes among French domestics just
alluded to. A mere desire for luxury would
not be liable to develop in one never at any

time of life exposed to its enervating influence, as the mass of working-women spring from parents who are also toilers, so that we may safely conclude that want, or a personal pride to appear better than others in the same station, is the most active cause of crime among underpaid women who have inherited no criminal taint.

The massing of large numbers of women at manufacturing centres is a circumstance from which spring many conditions which render the minor degrees of crime easy of commission. It is a singular fact that a great preponderance of numbers in one sex over the other, unrestrained by ties of family, and without the natural dependence of the different occupations and stations of life upon each other, almost invariably defines a locality in which the various forms of crime exist to excess. This has long been remarked of places in which the number of men greatly exceeds the number of women, but little attention has been called to the same condition as resulting from the preponderance in numbers of the other sex. Any one who has inquired into the causes of the social evil must have been struck by the numbers who admitted they had taken the first steps of their career in the populous manufacturing towns where an excessive number of their own sex was employed. There is this marked difference: an excess in the number of men leads to an increase of crimes against persons, while an excess of women increases crimes against property, in both cases relatively as to sex. I see no way, in our present knowledge of the subject, of explaining this, other than that a healthy tone of society demands an even balance of the different occupations and stations, and the presence of those ties of kinship which act so powerfully as restraints. Aside from these conditions I know of no facts which show that an even proportion in numbers of the sexes has a mutually conservative effect upon morals.

Generally, those in whom there is no inherited criminal taint, or no development of the criminal habit, would not seek nor create an opportunity for offense. But this can hold true only as to crimes against property, for in the other class of offenses, revenge, jealousy, avarice, and other emotions, may act suddenly as the exciting cause.

It is evident that woman's opportunities for crime are restricted by her relations to society, except, as we have already seen, certain facilities are afforded by her occupation. The moral influence of woman upon society is powerful; but it is negative rather than positive. Woman wields a sort of moral inhibitory power. Except as she may directly incite the other sex to crime, relationship to woman restrains and tones down the more salient points of the male character. Her lessened opportunity for crime results naturally from her sexual relations. Opportunity springs from the free mingling of large numbers in the heat and action of life. It is the antagonism between interests and objects, the friction, as it were, between the rapidly-moving actors, which brings out the intensity of emotion which results in the open or secret warfare of society. The vast majority of women are, to a certain extent, removed by the restraints not by any means artificial, but those which naturally result from their sexual relations, from the opportunity for crime. But I would limit even those restraints to crimes against property, rather than against persons. Although the ratio is sixteen and thirty-two to one hundred for each of these classes respectively, yet I believe it can be shown that the diminished ratio for crimes against persons depends upon other and more specific causes than her sexual attitude to society. Domesticity in this relation shows its potency as a conservator of morals; but,

standing alone and unaided by mutual
dependence and interest, its power is limited
to placing each subject beyond the more
closely besetting opportunities to which men
are exposed. It is but necessary to call
attention to the fact that it is from among
female domestics and operatives that the
ranks of prostitution are recruited, in order
to show that domesticity, which is the
condition of seven-eighths of the female
population, must be accompanied by other
relations in order to act as a more or less
complete restraint to crime. I use the word
here in its broadest possible sense, as
defining the position of the majority of the
sex. Great as the influence of the domestic
relation is, it is limited by the fact that it is
not permanent. It is constantly exposed to
those accidents to which all human relations
are liable. The passions and discordant
interests find in this relation a field for their
utmost activity. The sexual relation, which is
founded in the passions common to us all,
finds in them the elements of its strength and
permanency, as well as its weakness. It is
created and made lasting as life, or as brief
as a summer's day, by one and the same
organic emotion. Otherwise marriage, which
we may assume as the type of domesticity,
would not seem of itself to exist as a factor
in crime. As we study marriage in relation to

crime in another part of this paper, we shall perceive some very singular facts in which its bearings upon society are not so healthy as might be expected. It cannot be charged, however, to marriage, which is the most perfect of all human relations, but to its underlying weakness, the changing sexual conditions upon which it is based. It is safe in a broad grouping of crime to say that the emotions and passions define offenses against persons, while those against property are characterized by processes of mental calculation and deliberation. The last needs opportunity and temptation; the first exists everywhere. The domestic relation affords a refuge to the one, and contains within itself the element of the other. For these reasons I believe that the restraint afforded by domesticity must be mainly limited to crime against property.

In connection with this division of our subject we are brought face to face with the fact that women are as capable of crime as men. "It is not the degree of crime which keeps a woman back," says Quetelet.... "Since parricides and wounding of parents are more numerous than assassinations, which again are more frequent than murder, and wounds and blows generally, it is not simply weakness, for then the ratio for parricide and wounding of parents should be the same as for murder and wounding of strangers."[8]

With opportunities equal to man's, with the way to crime made easy, instead of being hedged in by the limits of her occupations, woman may equal him in the tendency to crime. Infanticide, in view of the strength of woman's maternal emotions, of the acuteness of her sympathies, and the general attributes of her character, stands alone as a crime in its relations to the sex. Considering the violence done to emotions which are a part of her organic psychical life, it has no equivalent in degree in the range of crime. If we apply to it the theory that the degree of offense, to a certain extent, affords a measure of the tendency to crime in the individual, this crime would reveal in women such a tendency greatly in excess of the other sex. But we must bear in mind that this crime, more than any other, which tends to make woman appear unduly prominent as a criminal, is a natural outgrowth of social surroundings. It is a marked instance of the fact that society contains within itself, even in its normal conditions, the moral agencies that create crime. Society has raised for itself a gauge of conduct, by which the alternative may be presented to any woman, of either crime or disgrace. At the same time society has so organized itself that the chief aim of every woman has been to establish a permanent relation to some man based upon involuntary sexual emotions. So long has this been in existence, so much power has it acquired by the increment of the forces of heredity, that it has become an organic law of society. This is a factor which enters into every woman's existence; by it her sexual life is made to exceed in intensity the intellectual. Ceaseless indwelling upon what every woman is taught to regard as both a necessity and an honor has tended to give undue force to every thing that relates both mentally and physically to her sexual existence. This is the manner in which society has made the way easy for woman's sexual error. Reflecting upon this, I confess to admiration for a sex which in the face of these difficulties has ever maintained such a well-deserved reputation for purity, and shown us that mankind turns instinctively to good rather than evil. Punishment is part of the crime, with society. To women for a sexual offense it measures out a punishment relentless and life-long. They are banished and hang on the outermost skirts of the inexorable law-giver as "Scarlet Letter" ones, for whom, in all their lives, there is no further hope.

Prepared in this fashion for infanticide, can it be wondered at that the ratio for this crime is 1,320 women to 100 men?[9] It is clearly an alternative of either social banishment and a total defeat of her selected destiny, or an attempt to conceal her error by crime. With an obliteration of one set of moral feelings there must be necessarily a weakening of the general moral character. She is therefore prepared to violate all the emotions and consciousness which have their origin in the very condition, through the undue development of which she met disaster. Infanticide appeal's to the woman's consciousness less formidable and repellent than her certain punishment by society. Her training has prepared her to place this lessened value upon the crime. Quetelet gives prominence to shame as an impelling motive to the crime. I can give it no such value. That sense of shame or modesty which exists as a phase of sexual cerebration in every mentally healthy woman, and that induces her to guard so jealously the casket after the jewel has been stolen or rather bestowed, is the part of her mental life to which the most violence has been done by her social error. What the French philosopher ought to refer to, is not the sexual quality of shame, but a sense of degradation which is common in an equal degree to both sexes. It is the sense that the good opinion of those we know, and whose esteem we value, has been forfeited. When we connect this sense of forfeiture with the fact that the interests in life which women are educated to hold most sacred, await but detection to be lost forever, I think we have found sufficient reason why this crime, which so antagonizes all womanly qualities, should exist to such a degree as to alter nearly one-half the ratio of the sexes in relation to crimes which involve human life. In analyzing the circumstances which bear upon infanticide, we are studying the darkest page of woman's criminal history. It proves that under a sufficient motive, and with every opportunity which her peculiar relation to that offense gives, she demonstrates her capacity to equal man in both the degree and number of her criminal acts. It is, however, an offense so characteristically entwined with her sexual life, and with her relations to society, that we must have a due regard for circumstances in contrasting it with any crime or series of crime in men. As already perceived, I am disposed in this inquiry to assign it but one value: her disposition to entertain the criminal idea, and under favorable opportunity to give that idea expression. In other respects the crime

29

stands alone, and can be used only in contrasting woman against woman. There are certain abnormal states of sexual cerebration connected with this offense which will more readily present themselves when we study the crime against society— the social evil.

In considering the effect of married or celibate life upon women in relation to crime, we are beset by many difficulties in regard to data. The officials upon whom devolve the duty of collecting criminal statistics, have yet to learn that they deprive their labor of much of its scientific usefulness by their errors of omission. The information has but little value that so many male or female criminals are married or unmarried. A proper study of the subject requires that this information be given in its relation to crime as it affects persons or property, the age at which the criminal career began in the two classes respectively, and crime among the widowed or divorced. Nearly all these facts are wanting. We can, however, collect sufficient data to enable us to shadow forth the probable truth in regard to this important matter. We may safely term marriage the unit of force in our present civilization. I have briefly called attention to its innate strength and weakness, which are inseparable from human mutability. It is easy to perceive the manner in which marriage may act as a conservator of morals, and its operation as a promoter of crime is equally evident; but the extent of its operation in either direction is difficult if not impossible to measure. In the examination of the returns of crime for the years 1867, 1871, and 1873, in New York City,[10] and which show great uniformity in the social condition of the sexes, we are met with the strange fact that the percentages of the married of both sexes correspond, being thirty-nine per centum; while for males the percentage of the unmarried is fifty-five, and for females in the same social condition it is forty-two. Regarding marriage as a conservator of morals in its affirmative rather than its negative relation, this statement places man on a level with woman; but observing further that the excess of male criminals is furnished from the unmarried, and that the single and married female criminals exist in nearly equal proportions, we can reach but one conclusion, that marriage exists as a restraining influence against crime more strongly among men than women. I think this result is opposed to the preconceived opinion of the majority, of the effect of marriage upon women. Marriage for women

31

has ever been regarded as a preliminary condition to reform. This is the result of the sentimentalism which has entered into the solution of many social problems. Marriage is not unmixed good. Lecky says of it, that "beautiful affections which had before been latent are evoked in some particular forms of union, while other forms of union are particularly fitted to deaden the affections, and pervert the character."[11] Woman's keenly emotional nature is well disposed to be exalted or depraved by marriage. It seems hardly possible to reach the true causes of the nearly negative results of marriage upon the morality of women by a study of the character of this sex alone. In women, rather than men, are mirrored the lights and shadows of society. Mentally she is the plastic material which takes its form from the protean phases of life around her. She is spiritually the resultant of her moral atmosphere. I believe these influences are more potent in forming her character than man's, from the nature of her dependent circumstances. With man's opportunity for objective life, he can remove himself, partly at least, from the moral surroundings; and by identifying himself both bodily and mentally with labor, which has for its object, usually, something to be attained in the future, he has loop-holes to escape from impressions received from others, which with a more subjective life would result in introspection, by which the mind is familiarized with the criminal idea.

From the same source we may gain additional facts as to the negative effect of marriage upon the morality of women. In the tables referred to, involving in the aggregate an excess of males over females of about two to one, we find the number of widowed females over males in the same social state to be nearly double. It is impossible to state specifically the nature of the crimes involved in this excess; but it probably represents, in a great measure, offenses against property. The social condition of widowhood in the average woman is not conducive of morality; and yet we have already shown that actual marriage is attended with nearly negative results. From this we may gain an idea of the extent to which women are the victims of circumstances at the beginning of their criminal career. The figures we have been analyzing represent crime in a great city. Under this condition, the excess in the number of widows represents probably cases of complete destitution. The fact that this excess of widows had no means of coping with this difficulty, except by a resort to

crime against property, renders the
conclusion safe that not only marriage had
not developed in them a condition favorable
to morality, but had actually so lowered the
moral tone as to render them unfit, as a
class, to contend with the difficulties of life,
and exhibit the same degree of morality as
the unmarried woman. Much of this result
must depend upon the unavoidable social
position of the married woman—one not at
all calculated to test either her morality or
self-reliance. The duties of maternity and
domesticity inseparable from her position,
do not fortify her against evil in her changed
relation to society. On the contrary, with the
burden of children upon her, in the time of
need, she looks upon crime less as a positive
than as a comparative evil. With the true
woman, there is no chance for hesitation in
the choice between crime in its minor forms
and her maternal feelings. But the marriage
relation has other influences in forming
woman's character as a criminal. The
intimacy of the wife with a bad husband,
who, if not a criminal, at least may be
capable of infusing lax moral notions in the
wife, would, if she were left a widow, surely
bear fruit. We need a more intimate
knowledge of many facts in order to fully
understand this question of widowhood in its
relation to crime. It is doubtful if returns of

crime from less densely populated places than New York City would furnish results at all parallel to those in relation to widows. The most plausible explanation I can give is, that these figures represent cases of absolute destitution.

There are many other relations that marriage bears to woman's career as a criminal, but which are beyond the scope of a magazine article., All that relates to infanticide, and the prevalence of the crime of the period, among the single and married, ought, I believe, in writings of a popular character, to be omitted, except possibly the grave words of warning. Upon this subject I have written all that I thought prudent several years ago, and to which I refer the reader.[12] The well-known lines of Pope upon the effect of familiarity with vice, are certainly very true to-day. It is by a too familiar view of even the shadow of crime, that in certain minds the criminal idea may be developed. We need but abolish the mental barriers to crime to step from the criminal idea to the criminal act.

Instinctive recoil from the criminal idea without any mental reservation is the characteristic of moral health. It is upon the morally healthy minds that unfavorable

35

social conditions may have most deplorable effect. One in whom the tendency to crime exists as a latent mental quality, requires no social conditions for its development. Whatever his or her occupation or social condition may be, this latent quality is liable to assume active existence, and shape the destiny of the individual. There is one quality that the criminal exhibits which defines him as a class, and is the only trait by the existence of which he becomes the member of a class. This is the liability, after the first outbreak, to commit repeated offenses. I find no term which expresses this so well as that of the criminal habit. Mentally and physically we are the victims of custom. Existence, like running streams, has a tendency to find for itself fixed channels. Life as it expands seems to seek points of least resistance for its outlets, and in following which it encounters less friction to retard its flow. In relation to crime, this exists as strongly as the opium or alcohol habit. The habit may find its factor in perverted moral feeling, whether hereditary or acquired, but its physical expression becomes the rule of life. Take such an instance as that of Ruloff, to whom Nature had given the crude material of a magnificent mind. In spite of the terrible potency of his criminal ideas, a longing for a

nobler and higher life existed within him in
sufficient force to give direction to
considerable self-culture. He stole, and
would kill without remorse any one who
stood between him and his object, simply to
gain money to enable him to follow his
studies. His life took the direction of the
least resistance. That which existed in the
normal man as a sense of right or wrong,
and offered itself as an obstacle to wrong-
doing, had no place in this man's mental life.
The outgoings of his life in the direction of
least resistance, simply and naturally led
him to crime. Cerebral and bodily activities,
among the good and bad alike, follow the
channels in which they encounter the least
friction, either objectively or subjectively. It
is thus we have the parson and the thief. By
inherited traits, early training, occupation or
social condition, weak points may be created
in the barriers which surround the activities
of life, and when maturity is reached the
individual's existence is defined by
ineffaceable lines. At this stage of life,
efforts, made either from within or without,
to give a new direction to these channels,
come too late. Habit has been established
which confirms the direction life has taken.
These two forces united seem irresistible. I
was, several years ago, brought in contact
with an instance which proves this. Lena

37

S—— was of German descent, and about fifty years old. She was of more than average intelligence, and of spare, nervous temperament. Lena was an instance of sporadic crime, in the sense that she did not belong to a criminal family. She followed the specialty of shoplifting, one that requires great coolness and cunning. Caught in the act and arrested, her history was brought out. She was married, and her husband was serving out a term of imprisonment, but with whom she had not lived for many years. She wandered from city to city, following her business; she had been repeatedly arrested, and more than once punished, and every time her whereabouts was brought to the knowledge of her family by her arrest, attempts were made to reclaim her, but in vain. Sentenced to several years of imprisonment, she quickly began to droop. She passed sleepless nights, with quick, irritable pulse, and loss of appetite. She constantly brooded, and laid more than one plot to escape, one of which was nearly successful. Out of about a year and a half of confinement, not more than a month of light labor was exacted of her. Her health became so broken that, at the earnest solicitation of her relatives, the prison authorities took the case up, and secured her a pardon on condition that she left the State, and her relatives provided for her. But the transition from prison-life to the comforts of a home, and a life of ease, offered no attractions to the unfortunate woman. I believe she remained under the care of her relative—a devoted sister—but a few months, when she resumed, out of choice, her old mode of life, and is now serving out another sentence.

This case shows how irresistibly the deliberate acts of life flow in the channel which habit and mental traits mark out for them. The barriers which society, and fear of punishment, and love, place in the way of a career like this of Lena S——, are swept away, as it were, before a flood. This is the destiny of the fatalist, and the force of habit, an expression of the theory of least resistance, and the effects of heredity of the sociologist. Let us analyze the last case further, to illustrate the theory of least resistance, as modified by occupation and social condition. It presents a seeming contradiction. She moved on in her career of crime late in life, with her moral atmosphere charged with resistance to her progress. Contrasted with this was her criminal pupilage in early life. Her husband united pauperism and crime, and if originally her moral perceptions were clear—which I doubt—she thus found the best school to

39

obscure these, and familiarize her with the criminal idea. With these faculties blunted and weakened, which serve to hedge in the impulses to evil, she proceeded to supply her wants by the method most familiar and easy. The thief looks upon the property of others in a peculiar way, and one that constitutes the essence of the crime. He believes in a sort of ownership which is mutual, and depends upon possession. This belief may become a fixed habit of mind. Originally it may have been easier to steal than to work, later it may become more impossible to work than to steal. Then came attempts at reform, made by others, with the life of ease and comfort, but the criminal grew wretched and drooped. There was but one life before her which met the demands of her nature— that was to wander from place to place and steal. This woman answered in no sense to the legal definition of the insane; she was not irresponsible for her acts, she knew their nature and the punishment which followed detection; but she simply did that which the most of us desire to do, follow the easier and pleasanter life. It has become the fashion of late to speak of criminals of this class as insane, but this theory cannot explain their irreclaimable condition. The real state, as it appears to me, is, that thoughts and acts move in the direction of least resistance.

What began in this way, may be confirmed
by habit, so that life may wear for itself
channels from which it is impossible that its
current may be driven.

1.


* "History of Civilization in England," vol.
i., pp. 22, 23.
* "History of European Morals from
Augustus to Charlemagne," vol. i., p. 157.
* Quetelet, "A Treatise on Man," p. 70.
* "Woman," from the French of M.
Michelet, by J, W. Palmer. New York, 1874.
* Quetelet, *loc. cit.*, p. 91.
* "Rapport au Roi," 1829.
* *Loc. cit.,* p. 85.
* *Loc. cit.,* p. 91.
* Quetelet, *loc. cit.*
* Table "B" 23d and 27th, and Table "A,"
29th, "Annual Reports of the Prison
Association, State of New York."
* *Loc. cit.* vol. ii., p. 369.
* "The Detection of Criminal Abortion, and
a Study of Fœticidal Drugs." James
Campbell, Boston, 1872.

# THE RELATIONS OF WOMEN TO CRIME.

## By
## ELY VAN DE WARKER, M. D.

II.

I SHALL, in this paper, consider briefly the sexual and other physical and mental conditions which modify woman's relations to crime. These conditions (*B*) mainly depend upon—1. Age; 2. Heredity; 3. Physical; and 4. Mental sexual peculiarities. In a former paper of this series,[1] I believe I proved, beyond a doubt, that there are types of mind which are purely the outcome of sex, and which define the mental condition of the sexes. In that paper, criminal statistics were used to assist in establishing the fact of sexual mental differences. Here the method is reversed, and sexual mental traits are employed to explain the known differences in the extent and degree of crime existing among men and women. This will involve the use of some of the facts already considered. While it is true that the social conditions, which we have so briefly analyzed,[2] bear upon woman chiefly because she is as she is, yet they bear also upon the other sex. Many of the sexual conditions we shall study relate to women alone, and, therefore, in their criminal career, exist as a defining force. If, in the ordinary concerns of life, women exhibit mental traits which serve amply to distinguish them, and place limits to their

43

activity, not less in the tabulated histories of crime are the same distinctions and limits found.

1. Age materially influences the extent and degree of crime in both sexes. In relation to physical and functional development, age exists as a defining force. It appears to affect the criminal careers of the sexes in two ways: by permitting such a degree of bodily power to be reached as to render possible criminal acts in different degrees; and, the bodily powers remaining the same, the varying mental conditions produce changes in the force and direction of the criminal impulse. Each period of life, therefore, is characterized by degrees and qualities of crime which belong to it. In other words, certain phases of crime are perpetrated at one period of life in excess of any other period. These remarks do not apply to both sexes equally, for these periods do not correspond either as to age, or in the nature of the offense, the excess of which distinguishes one period from another.

For the purpose of studying the influence of age upon the criminal career of women, I shall analyze the figures of Mr. F. G. P. Neison.[3] The materials embraced in the table of Mr. Neison are for five years, from

1834 to 1839; for, strange to say, the Home-Office returns, since the year last named, to the date of Mr. Nelson's publication, ceased to give the age and sex with reference to classes of crime. In order to simplify the comparison, I shall take the number of male criminals corresponding in age to the female, as the standard of measurement in reference to any given division of crime. Fractions are omitted in reference to both sexes.

At twelve years of age and younger the proportion of females to males is 1 to 6 for crimes against persons, and for crimes against property without violence for the same age the proportion is again 1 to 6. Bearing in mind what has been said in a former chapter,[4] that the ratios of the sexes as to crimes against persons and property are 16 to 100 for the former, and 26 to 100 for the latter, and which also correspond to the difference in strength between the sexes, we see that the element of sexual inequality in strength does not present itself as a factor. In other words, the correspondence in the proportion of the sexes to the two classes of crime represents physical equality, while the difference (1 to 6) is the result of mental sexual traits, which, even at this early age, present themselves. During the next four years the proportion in reference to crimes against persons is nearly double, being 1 to 11; while against property the proportion decreases, being 1 to 5. The average physical strength of the sexes for the second period (twelve to sixteen years) is about equal, so that this sudden proportional increase in crimes against persons in the male sex is the result almost entirely of those qualities which mentally characterize the male. This conclusion is rendered nearly positive by the fact that the maximum is attained by the males in the next five years, sixteen to twenty-one, and is only 1 to 12, during which period it is that the greatest difference in strength between the sexes is developed; yet this difference is represented by an increase of only 1 in the proportion. This agrees with what we know of men, that the development of the passions keeps just in advance of the development of the physical strength, just as the strength declines in advance of the passions. Studying for a moment longer this second period of life (twelve to sixteen) we learn this important fact: that in woman's criminal career it is, proportionally with man, the best period in her life, for at this time also occurs the greatest difference in crimes against property, 1 to 5, the maximal difference in the sexes, as to crimes against persons, being reached at twenty-one years. For the periods following of ten years each, the proportion steadily decreases in the following order, 1 to 9, 1 to 7, until at the decade, between forty and fifty years, we reach again the proportion of childhood (1 to 6). Now, the inference is, not that men grow better and women worse; but that the period of greatest passional intensity has been passed, while in both sexes the will has attained its greatest force. In other words, the period of caution has been reached. This accords with the law that the greatest mental vigor corresponds with structural completion. That this explanation is plausible is shown by the fact that the last decade mentioned is the period in which the proportion between the sexes in crimes against property is more nearly equal, being 1 to 2 and a fraction, and which for former decades steadily held at 1 to 3. There is a further confirmation of this, in the fact that for two periods, fifty to sixty, and sixty and upward, crimes against persons increase among men; the proportion being 1 to 9 and 1 to 10 respectively. That this is not the result of any increase of morality in the other sex, the uniform ratio of the sexes for crimes against property, during the ages last named, renders probable. From the same source we may obtain information which tends to show the truth of the remark made by M. Quetelet, that the proportion of women as to men increases "according to the necessity of the greater publicity before the crime can be perpetrated."[5] In the division of crime called offenses against the currency, we have the conditions favorable to a more even proportion of the sexes. In an offense of this kind the physical equality is not involved. It becomes a question of secrecy, cunning, and shrewdness. These are mental qualities which exist with equal force in the sexes. Consequently in this division of crime for all ages we find a mean proportion of 1 to 2. Expressed in detail the proportion is equal in childhood, 1 to 2 at the next period, and 1 to 3 for the three following, until, at the decade between forty and fifty years, it drops to 1 to 2, and is equal again for the two following periods. The influences which cause equality in the proportions at the two extremes of ages are probably those which produce the same, or nearly the same, results in relation to the other orders of crime.

This analysis of Mr. Nelson's statistics reveals to us a very interesting period in the lives of both sexes—that between forty and fifty years. For all the classes of crime examined, we find the sexes at this period

48

proportionally approaching equality; being in two classes actually at that of childhood. These two classes of crime are those which involve the greatest violence, crimes against persons; and the least, crimes against the currency. For the first, I have already offered a reasonable explanation, that of the period of caution; but, in reference to the latter, we must search further, in order to get at a probable cause. In the last-named offense, we have as a characterizing mental trait the very condition which explains the decrease in the proportion for crimes against persons, and yet at the terminal periods of life we find it obeying the same law. There is one fact which forces itself upon the attention in connection with this; that the first approach to equality in the proportions of the sexes begins suddenly at the term of life between forty and fifty years. This period, for men especially, is that in which the forces engaged in structural repair and waste are in equilibrium. It is one of structural rest, but of functional activity. At no other period in the life of man, therefore, is he physically more competent to meet the demands of his mental life. With women, it is also a period of structural rest, linked to a state of functional completion, so far as the prime motive of sexual life is concerned. It appears reasonable, in view of this, that

49

physical factors be excluded as a probable cause of the phenomenon. But there exist valid reasons for exempting the male sex partly from the operation of the laws affecting this equalization in the proportion of the sexes. These reasons show presumptively that the subtile and obscure laws of crime operate more actively upon the female than the male sex; that, in obedience to these laws, her relations to crime are prolonged into periods of life when men are becoming, to a certain extent, exempt from their operations.

My friend Mr. R. L. Dugdale, of New York, in his brilliant study of the natural history of crime,[6] by an analysis of Tables I. and II. of Mr. Nelson,[7] arrives at important facts. In the tables referred to, crime is classified according to age, and percentages are calculated based upon the total population for each age specified. The maximum for male criminals is found in the period of twenty to twenty-five years, with a percentage to the total population of that age of .7702. Between fifty and sixty years the percentage drops to only .1694. The same law holds good for women, but with modified ratios. Comparing the two sexes, the following results are reached: the tendency to crime, as exhibited in its actual commission, for males at all ages until sixty, diminishes at the rate of 33.333 per centum. For females under similar conditions of age, it diminishes at the rate of 25 per centum. Keeping in view the liability to error in a search through the obscure underlying forces which seem to regulate human conduct in the aggregate, it nevertheless appears reasonable to expect an explanation of this phenomenon to lie in the physical rather than the mental conditions of the sexes at the terminal periods of life. In the decade which was above distinguished as that of physical equilibrium, the governing principles seemed to be the expression of mental forces; but, on reaching the sixtieth year of life, the conditions are reversed. While in the former the conditions of waste and repair were equal, in the latter the repair of the physical forces is exceeded by the waste. This is a law which applies equally to both sexes, but with this difference in the result: the occupation and the crimes which belong in such great excess to men are those which require more physical strength than the occupations and crimes which are adapted to the lesser strength of women. Let us take a familiar illustration: after a man at sixty years of age has retired from the scenes of his labor in the mine, or field, or workshop, the wife of the same age, or older, is yet profitably engaged in her lighter domestic duties. She is yet contributing as materially to the comforts of her family as during the more active years of the husband's life. Now, while it is quite evident that we must regard the cause of the sudden more near equality in the proportion of the sexes which presents itself in the period of life between forty and fifty years as due to psychical changes, the evidence is yet stronger that the ratio of the more rapid decrease of male criminals at the more advanced period of fifty to sixty years is due to the cause I have named—the rapid impairment of physical energy peculiar to the period. Since men greatly preponderate in those phases of crime which demand strength, belligerency, and publicity in the perpetration, the conclusion is legitimate that Crime would rapidly decrease at the time of life in which these qualities are wanting, or are impaired. If we examine the relation of men to the orders of crime, in the perpetration of which these qualities are not necessary, and in which strength may be replaced by caution, and belligerency by cunning, as in offenses against the currency, and in the sixth division of Mr. Nelson called "other offenses," embracing the lighter shades of criminal conduct, we shall see that the proportions between the sexes characteristic of earlier ages hold on unchanged through this last period of life.

It will be interesting to return for a moment and examine what are the real proportions of the sexes, during the criminally most active period of life, between twenty-one and thirty years. While we would not expect in this period to find the groundwork laid for criminal conduct, yet it is the term of life, in both sexes, in which the effects of heredity, of early training, assume activity, and give shape and color to the destiny of the individual. What goes before may be called the germ period, and this the period of fruition. The years which precede the meridional term of life are under the influence of structural and intellectual genesis. It is the result of an aggregation of forces tending to a common end. Life has not reached the level of the conflicting emotions, passions, and activities, which at the completion of structure exist so potently. Activity at this period is the expression of simple laws, which lead to a uniform result. Mr. Neison, reasoning purely from statistics, arrives at the same conclusion, that "in the juvenile period of life the tendency to crime is under the influence of more constant laws or elements, and therefore shows less fluctuation than in mature life."[8] The same conclusions hold good at the closing years of life. Youth and old age unite in the degree and quality of crime. The aggregate of crime in general is committed at the earlier part of this intermediate period of both sexes. The crime of this decade of life is more than quadruple that of any other. During this period occur those differences in the tendency to crime between the sexes which affect the total results. During this period, sex powerfully asserts its influence. Sex is no longer existing potentially in incomplete structure; but it is partly the sum of completed structural effort. Psychically, it is emotion, passion, and unconscious cerebral activity. Physically, it is the difference in development and mechanical power. Each of these is a factor in the differences real and apparent in the tendency to crime existing between men and women. There are many other causes, some of the more important of which have already been referred to, and are of social rather than sexual origin. But social factors operate more strongly at this period than at any other. Society in all its phases is made up of the activities of this period of life. Those forces which in their totality express all there is of society, seem to concentrate and coincide with those forces which express all there is of sex, and tend to one period of life common to both men and women.

2. In this connection it is proper to examine the bearings of women to the hereditary tendency to crime. Recent study of the relations of sex to crime has shown that the hereditary element in the criminal tendency may assume sexual phases. This is exemplified by the law of movement in the direction of the least resistance. The hereditary taint being a fixed factor, it assumes expression in acts which are most in accord with sexual peculiarities. This is nearly equivalent to Dr. Carpenter's theory of special mental aptitudes as giving direction to the force of habit;[9] except that its operation is extended to the hereditary transmissions of mental or physical qualities. It is only in the early middle period of life that, from the nature of things, we would expect to find the criminal tendency under the complete sway of sexual life. The inherited criminal tendency in childhood and early youth finds its outlet in a viciousness common to both sexes, or in the milder forms of crimes against property. This is asserted on general principles. Dr. Carpenter remarks that "this diversity may be in a great part attributed to changes in the physical constitution. Thus, the sexual

feeling, which has a most powerful influence on the direction of the thoughts in adolescence, adult age, and middle life, has comparatively little effect at the earlier and later periods."[10] This also accords with Mr. Dugdale's theory of criminal analogues. This theory, in his important work,[11] is mainly brought out in relation to the entailment of crime, and its truth lies in the fact that, in the same family of criminals, while the males are thieves, the females are prostitutes—one the equivalent or analogue of the other. The same family, in the two extremes of life, childhood and old age, exhibits pauperism as either the reality or promise of a criminal career. From the fact that pauperism exists as a parasite upon productive society, and preys upon society to its permanent injury, and makes no return, it will be regarded in this paper as an equivalent to crime against property. When we consider that criminals by entailment are exposed to environments possessing essential qualities in common, it is reasonable to expect that in such crime would conform in a more regular manner to those laws which seem to govern moral conduct, than in those who drift into crime through impulse or misfortune. This, in a general sense, holds true. M. Prosper Despine, in his "Psychologic Naturelle," shows that incendiarism exists in the young of both sexes with the inherited taint, as a characteristic. M. Despine brings out with great force a mental condition of those who inherit crime that gives an additional cause for the operation of the laws of crime with almost undeviating regularity upon this class. This is the total or nearly total absence of the moral sense—moral idiocy—which isolates the offspring of criminal families from the children of untainted birth. By this moral blindness they are distinguished throughout their lives. Thus there are wanting in this class the moral elements which effect or impede the criminal tendency in others. The sense of right or wrong, the sense of shame or disgrace, in no way interferes with the criminal tendency. This is the very condition necessary for the unembarrassed operation of Mr. Dugdale's very probable law of criminal analogues or equivalents. Hence we may say, with almost positive certainty, that the children of both sexes, with the inherited taint, are paupers; that adult life in the male is distinguished by pauperism and crime; that adult life in the female is devoted to prostitution, and that old age brings both sexes again to the state of pauperism. And here again we encounter the phenomenon revealed by an analysis of Mr. Nelson's statistics: the criminal equivalent existing between childhood and

57

senility. It is childhood and old age joining hands, as it were, over the fevered and crime-laden middle life. But, while the moral faculties are absent, the mental powers are perverted to an equal degree. Any one accustomed to closely observe confirmed criminals must be cognizant of the fact that they are not as other men in their habits of mind. What one observes may not be called insanity, in the full meaning of the word, but it appears to be a departure from the standard one forms from mingling with average men. I have noticed this especially with regard to women. From an experience of two years with criminal women undergoing punishment in the Onondaga Penitentiary, I cannot recall an instance in which mental traits were wanting to distinguish them from the average woman. In this class mental peculiarities may be intensified into actual insanity, and the tendency to it exist stronger than in any other class. M. Ribot[12] shows that hereditary crime and insanity are closely connected, and refers to Drs. Ferrus and Lélut, who have established the great frequency of insanity among criminals. Dr. Bruce Thompson, in a recent work,[13] supports this by figures, and proves that twelve per centum of insanity occurs among prisoners, with fifty per centum of recommittals, revealing the strength of the inherited tendency.

The two more important inherited criminal traits which reveal sexual types in their development are pauperism and prostitution. Pauperism appears to be as characteristic of the male sex as prostitution is of the female. The ratio of sexes receiving relief is twenty per cent, of men to thirteen per cent, of women, in out-door, and thirteen per cent, of men to 9.5 per cent, of women in almshouse relief. De Marsangy fixes the ratio at seven times more vagabondage among men than women.[114] As a rule, women receive relief—if single—while child-bearing, and if married they follow the condition of the husband; while widows drift back into prostitution. "Thus we find," remarks Mr. Dugdale, "that although the rates of wages are lower for women, charity is much more frequent among men."[15] The above relates to those who are known to receive relief. The hereditary strength of the last-named offense is shown by the Juke family, so carefully studied by Mr. Dugdale—52.4 per cent, of the women following prostitution. If hereditary disease accompanies the entailment of crime, pauperism is a matter of course; the subject rarely attaining the rank of a criminal, except in the most petty of the

offenses against property. Pauperism is a
condition of effeteness. It represents the
dregs which drop downward through the
several strata of society. Morally, it is the
most negative condition of humanity. The
pauper has sunk below the level of crime.
He abstains from crime, not by moral
restraints, but by inertness. The woman with
the same taint has sunk below the level of
the active phases of crime. She drifts into
harlotry because it is easier than to steal. If
disabled, she becomes a pauper, and thus
oscillates between the almshouse and the
brothel—a passionless, nerveless being, with
all the normal energies crushed out under
the burden of entailed defects.

3. It is a more difficult matter to trace
through the complicated net-work of
passions, emotions, and motives, which
underlies the degrees and varieties of crime,
the purely sexual physical factor. The main
difficulty consists in discriminating this
from 'the mental sexual differences which
may exist as a cause of differentiation in
crime. It is essential, if possible, to gain an
approximate idea of the limits of these
differences. With the present data at
command, this can be accomplished only in
the most superficial manner. There exists
here more than the suspicion of a great law,

the operation of which, if fully known, would clear up many of the doubts lingering around this important subject. While the physical differences will serve to explain the varying relations of the sexes to crime in their broader and more superficial aspects, the mental sexual traits will serve to define the differences in motives, tendencies, and innate moral proclivities of the sexes. Instead of being satisfied with the simple explanation, that the extent of man's excess over woman as a criminal represents the excess of woman over man as a moral being, this knowledge would show that this is not a question of comparative morality alone, but one of intellectual equivalents. To study carefully the scope of the moral equivalents of the sexes is to reach the relations of things in their genesis. It is in this way that the relations of the sexes socially, as well as in crime, will be taken out of the realm of sentimentalism and placed upon a basis of fact. Sentimental views of the relationship of women to crime exist so generally, that they act as a force in the way of an unbiased investigation of the subject. Take, for instance, such a writer as M. de Marsangy,[16] whose motive is the serious one of the amelioration of the penal laws in their bearings upon women, who gravely concludes that man has a "nature less noble, less delicate, less perfect than woman," and yet quotes approvingly that, "*Das Weib ist Engel oder Teufel.*" It is this personal bias which has hitherto obscured this subject, and rendered the work of such writers as M. de Marsangy useless for scientific purposes. Fortunately, this style of scientific writing belongs to the French school of both sentiment and morals.

The mental reflex result of physical strength, as expressed in the criminal act, is more clearly shown in crimes against property attended with violence. Distinguishing it from the other orders of crime—malicious offenses against property, and offenses without violence—we have the motive in the first-mentioned class narrowed to the desire of possession, but so associated with the consciousness of personal strength that it is employed as an agent of the crime. Belligerency, revenge, and other emotions which tend to crime, are absorbed in the order of malicious offenses, and thus the field is left clear, in the class under analysis, for the full play of the physical factor. Omitting ages under sixteen years, as being too nearly equal physically in the sexes, and basing our proportion on the number of criminals of both sexes from that age to twenty-one years, the proportion is 1 woman to 18 men, while for the ten years following it is 1 to 20.[17] This is twice the proportion between the sexes for crimes against persons, and seven times that for crimes against property without violence, for corresponding ages. When we contrast this with the fact that the mean proportion between the sexes for all crimes against property is 1 to 4, and for crimes against the person it is 1 to 6, we may form an idea of the enormous influence of physical strength as a restraint to woman's criminal tendencies. We have, however, to modify this somewhat, by giving more or less value to woman's tendency to avoid those crimes which require publicity in both the planning and perpetration, and which is implied in violent crimes against property; but even giving this trait due weight, the physical factor as exhibited in this order of crime is the one which, more than any other, defines its character. While woman's deficient physical strength, compared to man's, acts so powerfully as an obstacle in the division of crime just considered, it is highly probable that in other offenses it also acts in the same manner, varying in amount, as this quality is necessary to the successful perpetration of the crime. In those crimes in which this factor does not enter, we at once notice that the ratios of the sexes approximate. In adultery, for instance, the proportion of the sexes is about the same.[18] In infanticide, I have already remarked on the ease with which women enter upon a criminal course, when this conforms to the direction of purely sexual qualities; and, undoubtedly, intensity is added by the absence of physical strength as a requisite to the perpetration of the crime. In crimes against the currency, the same near equality in the number of the sexes involved may be noticed, and the fact that the proportions for the most active period of adult life and for childhood and old age are about the same renders it highly probable that this equality is accounted for by the physical strength required for its perpetration being possessed equally by the sexes. In crimes against persons, the influence of this factor can be traced, but not in so marked a manner as in the crimes referred to. In poisoning, for instance, the ratio between the sexes is 91 women to 100 men,[19] and while active mental traits may in part exist as causes for this nearly equal ratio of the sexes, yet the total absence of any need of physical strength must be given due value. Poison is essentially a weapon of weakness. It figures largely in history as the agent of women and politicians. One reason, which probably existed in mediæval days, but which cannot be regarded in modern times, was the difficulty of detection in cases of death by poisoning. It was surrounded by an atmosphere of horrible suspicion, which was never relieved by certainty. It was selected as a political agent by reason of this secrecy, by both sexes, and thus at this period had no sexual qualities. Modern advances in chemistry have rendered poisoning one of the most surely detected of all crimes, and its perpetration has become a characteristic of the weak and cowardly. In some other offenses, as in incendiarism, in which physical strength is as unessential as in poisoning, the ratio between the sexes falls to 34 in 100. Although this is a crime well within the compass of woman's physical abilities, yet it involves other elements, which deter women from its perpetration. Motive, which is the exciting cause of crime and enters largely into the intensity of the tendency, cannot act so powerfully in the latter as the former crime. In order to kill, a stronger motive is required than to burn. Incendiarism requires considerable personal exposure, and danger of immediate detection. Parricide with a ratio of 50 to 100, and wounding of parents with a ratio of 22 to 100 (Quetelet), offer a remarkable contrast to murder and the wounding of strangers, with a ratio taken together of 9 to

100. The necessity of physical strength exists equally in the perpetration of these crimes. The marked difference in ratio, therefore, must be explained by other means. Opportunity and domesticity, already referred to in a former paper, exist largely as the cause of the difference. M. Quetelet, speaking in general terms of the influence of opportunity and domestic habits upon woman's criminal career, remarks: "They can only conceive and execute guilty projects on individuals with whom they are in the greatest intimacy; thus, compared with man, her assassinations are more often in her family than out of it." It would be difficult to present a stronger argument of the influence of woman's social position as a restraint to crime. As we observe in the crimes just referred to, it is not the enormity of the offense which restrains, for we have in parricide twelve times the frequency of murder; it is not weakness, for then parricide, murder, and wounding, should agree in frequency. We are able to trace in this no influence of morality, it is simply the result of the varying degrees of opportunity, domestic life, and mental peculiarities.

1.

• POPULAR SCIENCE MONTHLY, JULY, 1875.

• Popular Science Monthly, November, 1875.

• "Contributions to Vital Statistics," table xxix., London, 1857.

• Popular Science Monthly, November, 1875.

• *Loc. cit.,* p. 90.

• "Thirtieth Annual Report of the Prison Association, State of New York," p. 179.

• *Loc. cit,* pp. 303, 304.

• *Loc. cit.,* p. 407.

• "Principles of Mental Physiology," p. 374.

• *Loc. cit.,* p. 365.

• "Thirtieth Report," etc., p. 146.

• "Heredity," p. 29.

• "The Hereditary Nature of Crime."

• "Étude sur la Moralité comparée de la Femme et de l'Homme," par M. Bonneville de Marsangy.

• *Loc. cit.,* p. 161.

• *Loc. cit.,* p. 133.

• Neison, *loc. cit.*

• De Marsangy, *loc. cit.*

19.  •  Quetelet, *loc. cit.,* p. 91.

www.ingramcontent.com/pod-product-compliance
Lightning Source LLC
Chambersburg PA
CBHW061733250726
48657CB00002B/900